It can airdrop **TANKS** from its rear.

U.S. AIR FORCE

YJ

AF 74685

KEIKO, the orca from *Free Willy,* was flown to the movie set in a C-130.

3

The **inflatoplane** was designed in the **1950S** to be **airdropped** to pilots stuck behind enemy lines.

The plane could be inflated in **FIVE** minutes!

4

WHEN COMPACTED, IT COULD FIT IN A WHEELBARROW.

The Fokker DR.1 was a TRIPLANE: it had THREE wings!

No original Fokkers exist today. Only copies do.

THE RED BARON, THE MOST FEARED PILOT OF WORLD WAR I (1914–1918), FLEW A FOKKER.

The B-52 can drop or launch a wider variety of weapons than any other U.S. aircraft.

8

The B-52 has been in use since the 1940S.

THE B-1B CARRIES MORE GUIDED AND UNGUIDED WEAPONS THAN ANY OTHER U.S. MILITARY PLANE.

It can track, target, and engage moving vehicles in split seconds.

10

At sea level, the B-1B can fly

MACH 1.2!

That's almost twice the speed that a passenger jet flies.

THE HARRIER IS THE ONLY FIGHTER JET THAT CAN TAKE OFF AND LAND VERTICALLY.

12

THE JET CAN FLY MORE THAN 630 MILES PER HOUR (1,010 kilometers per hour)!

Its MASSIVE
turbofan engines
are made by
ROLLS-ROYCE.

The VALKYRIE BOMBER could fly MACH 3!

That's more than twice as fast as the B1-B bomber.

The plane was built to be a **LONG-RANGE NUCLEAR BOMBER,** but was never used for that purpose.

ONLY **TWO** VALKYRIE BOMBERS WERE EVER PRODUCED. ONLY ONE SURVIVES **TODAY.**

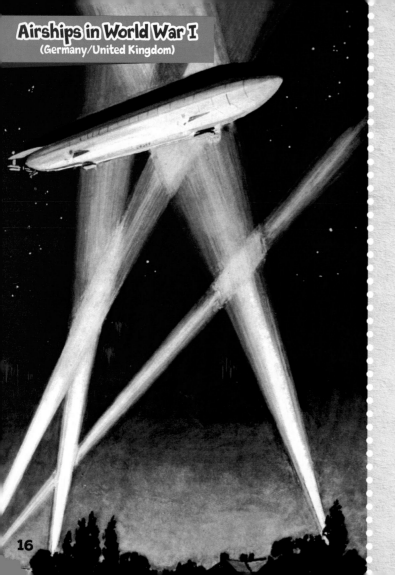

The British used **BLIMPS** as navy patrol ships.

They were used to spot and fire at German subs.

16

PARACHUTES WERE RARELY CARRIED ON AIRSHIP FLIGHTS AT THE BEGINNING OF THE WAR.

THEY WERE DEEMED UNNECESSARY.

ALMOST 6,000 BEAUFIGHTERS WERE BUILT BETWEEN 1940 AND 1946.

THE BEAU WAS CALLED "WHISPERING DEATH" BY THE JAPANESE BECAUSE THE ENGINES WERE SO QUIET.

Its quiet ENGINES and RADAR SYSTEM made this plane a stealthy nighttime fighter.

The **KIOWA** was the first army helicopter to have an all-glass cockpit.

KIOWAS can be armed with HELLFIRE MISSILES, HYDRA 70 ROCKETS, STRINGER MISSILES, OR MACHINE GUNS.

THE OH-1 IS QUICK AND STEALTHY.

Its nickname is THE NINJA.

It can fly 168 miles per hour (270 kph)!

IT HAS TANDEM, OR SIDE-BY-SIDE, COCKPITS.

The ORION is considered the TOP maritime patrolling airplane in the world.

IT IS RESPONSIBLE FOR KEEPING OCEAN WATERS SAFE FROM ENEMIES.

It is used by **17** different countries and has a **16-HOUR** nonstop flytime.

THE PLANE IS SOMETIMES USED TO FIND MODERN DAY PIRATES.

LET'S COMPARE:

SOPWITH CAMEL

COUNTRY:	United Kingdom
YEAR MADE:	1917
NO. OF WINGS:	2
SPEED (MPH/KPH):	115/185
WEAPONS:	2 Vickers machine guns
RATE OF CLIMB:	1,085 feet (331 meters) per minute

WWI FIGHTER PLANES

VS. THE FOKKER D.VII

Germany

1918

2

117/188

2 Spandau machine guns

772 feet (235 meters)
per minute

LET'S COMPARE:

EARLY ATTACK HELICOPTER WITH FUTURE ATTACK HELICOPTER

COUNTRY:

YEAR IN SERVICE:

MAXIMUM SPEED (MPH/KPH):

MAXIMUM RANGE (MI/KM):

WEAPONS:

MIL-MI 24 (HIND)

Soviet Union

1973

208/335

99/159

machine guns/
rockets/missiles

SIKORSKY S-97 RAIDER

United States

2020

253/407

354/570

machine guns/
cannons/missiles

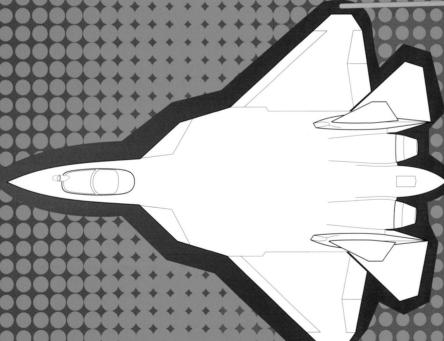

The T-50 is a large FIGHTER.

Its wingspan is about 50 FEET (15 M)!

It can reach **MACH 4** in just a few seconds.

That's over **3,000** miles per hour (4,830 kph)!

IT CARRIES ADVANCED X-74M2 CRUISE MISSILES.

THE F-15 IS A REMARKABLE AIRCRAFT IN EVERY WAY.

IT CAN LAND SAFELY WITH ONLY ONE WING!

IT HAS A PERFECT RECORD: ZERO AIR COMBAT LOSSES.

The F-15 can successfully shoot down satellites.

33

The B-2 is covered with a special paint that makes it almost invisible to ground-based sensors.

In 2003 JENNIFER WILSON became the first female pilot to fly the B-2 in a COMBAT MISSION.

ONE B-2 COSTS ABOUT $1.2 BILLION.

35

The Mustang was considered the BEST FIGHTER of WORLD WAR II (1939–1945)

because it could fly farther and faster than most of the other aircraft of the day.

MORE THAN 15,000 MUSTANGS WERE MADE.

Pilots from at least 25 DIFFERENT countries flew the Mustang.

DURING WORLD WAR II, MUSTANG PILOTS SHOT DOWN ALMOST 5,000 ENEMY AIRCRAFT.

The AEROCYCLE was designed in the 1950s to be a "FLYING PLATFORM."

A PILOT COULD STEER IT BY SIMPLY SHIFTING HIS WEIGHT.

THE PROJECT WAS CANCELED AFTER THERE WERE TOO MANY TESTING CRASHES.

The **ANTONOV AN-225** is the world's **LARGEST MILITARY TRANSPORT AIRPLANE.**

IT WAS BIG ENOUGH TO CARRY THE ROCKET BOOSTERS FOR THE SOVIET SPACE SHUTTLE.

IT IS 276 FEET (84 M) LONG.

That's longer than approximately five sperm whales lined up end to end!

The C-5 is America's largest WORKING CARGO AIRPLANE.

The paint alone weighs 2,600 pounds (1,179 kg)!

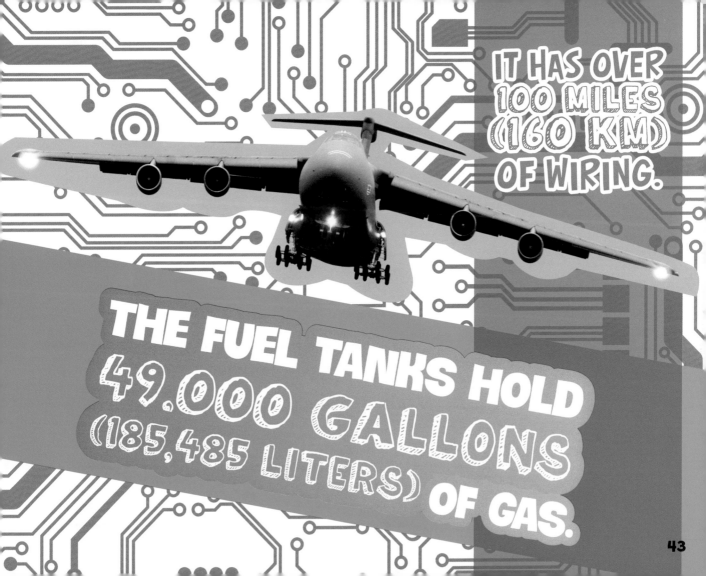

IT HAS OVER 100 MILES (160 KM) OF WIRING.

THE FUEL TANKS HOLD 49,000 GALLONS (185,485 LITERS) OF GAS.

CHINOOKS
are very rarely retired.
They are fixed instead.

The CH-47D model can lift
19,500 POUNDS (8,845 KG)!

One pilot who fought in AFGHANISTAN (2001-2014) flew the exact same CHINOOK his grandfather flew more than 50 YEARS earlier in the VIETNAM WAR (1959-1975).

The VOUGHT V-173 Was dubbed the "FLYING PANCAKE" for obvious reasons!

WHEN PEOPLE SAW THE V-173 FLYING, THEY THOUGHT IT WAS A UFO.

It was almost the first vertical-lifting aircraft to go into production. But it was scrapped due to funding issues.

The **HERON** is an aircraft **PILOTED BY REMOTE CONTROL.**

ON

IT IS USED FOR SPYING, SO IT DOESN'T CARRY ANY WEAPONS.

IT CAN FLY FOR **24 HOURS** AT A TIME.

The media called this aircraft "A MAMMOTH WATER SPIDER."

IT NEVER LEFT THE TESTING STAGES BECAUSE IT HAD TOO MANY UNRESOLVED PROBLEMS.

THE PILOT WHO FLEW IT SAID, "THE FLIGHT WAS LIKE RIDING A **POGO STICK** IN A SITTING POSITION— up, down, up, down."

The rotors were almost 130 feet (40 m) long! That's about as long as 16 horses all lined up.

SUKHOI T-50 STEALTH FIGHTER

F-15CJ/DJ

F-22A

SU-30MKV

SU-27SK

F-15K

 UNITED STATES

 CHINA

 SOUTH KOREA

 JAPAN

 VIETNAM

 RUSSIA

The **ATLANT** will be ready in **2018** and will combine **HOVERCRAFT, AIRPLANE, HELICOPTER,** and **AIRSHIP TECHNOLOGY** into one vehicle.

ITS ADVANTAGE TO A CARGO PLANE?

IT DOESN'T NEED A RUNWAY TO TAKE OFF.

IT CAN LAND OR TAKE OFF FROM ANYWHERE.

THIS AIRCRAFT, TESTED IN 1957–1960, WAS DUBBED "The Flying Jeep."

The pilot sat in the open air in a seat at the front of the aircraft.

IT TOPPED OUT AT 32 MILES PER HOUR (51 KPH).

THE FLYING JEEP WAS VERY EASY TO FLY, BUT IT COULDN'T GO HIGH ENOUGH, SO THE ARMY SCRAPPED IT.

This fighter jet didn't need a runway.
IT USED THE OCEAN!

IT HAD HYDRO-SKIS FOR TAKEOFF AND LANDING.

SEA DART WAS THE **FIRST** AND **ONLY** SEAPLANE TO EVER REACH **SUPERSONIC SPEEDS.**

SADLY, DURING ONE OF ITS TEST FLIGHTS, IT disintegrated. THE SEA DART WAS NEVER USED IN SERVICE.

McDonnell XF-85 Goblin (United States)

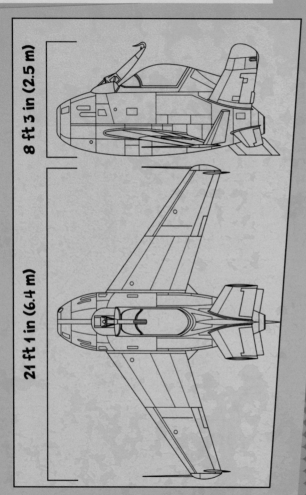

8 ft 3 in (2.5 m)

21 ft 1 in (6.4 m)

THE GOBLIN IS THE SMALLEST JET-PROPELLED FIGHTER EVER BUILT.

IT WAS MADE TO BE CARRIED AND LAUNCHED FROM A B-36 BOMBER.

The Goblin flew fine. But it had other problems, so it was cancelled.

THE LEDUC 010 RAMJET RODE PIGGYBACK ON ANOTHER PLANE FOR ITS FIRST FEW FLIGHTS.

After that, the Leduc 010 was the **first aircraft** to fly using only **ramjet power**.

THE LEDUC HAD A GLASS NOSE CONE THAT COULD ACT AS AN ESCAPE POD IN AN EMERGENCY.

During World War II, 430 civilian and Allied ships were sunk by U-boats.

U-BOATS WERE VERY COMPLICATED: THERE WERE AROUND 50 HANDWHEELS INSIDE USED TO MANAGE PRESSURE.

Most U-boats had emblems.
The U-47's was a snorting bull.

...The Story of the Doomed U-1206

The U-1206 started its first patrol in April of 1945.

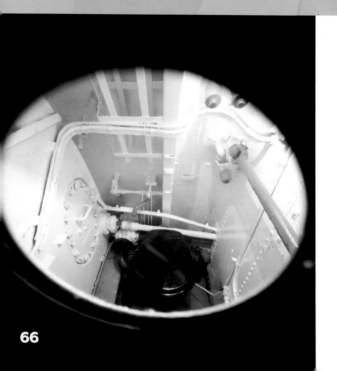

ON
APRIL 14,
THE COMMANDER WAS FORCED TO SURFACE THE SUB BECAUSE OF A
MALFUNCTIONING
TOILET.

L.A. class subs can vertically launch Tomahawk missiles.

THESE SUBS ARE PROPELLED BY NUCLEAR REACTORS.

ONE SUB COSTS ABOUT **$900 MILLION** DOLLARS TO BUILD.

L.A. CLASS SUBS WEIGH 6,900 TONS EACH!

BEFORE A SUBMARINE CAN DIVE, THE CREW HAS TO PERFORM MORE THAN 225 OPERATIONAL CHECKS.

U.S. NAVY

TUBE EMPTY

SUBS ARE PAINTED BLACK SO THEY CAN HIDE UNDERWATER FROM ENEMIES.

SUBS CAN DIVE MORE THAN 800 FEET (245 M). BUT EXACTLY HOW DEEP A SUB CAN DIVE IS CLASSIFIED INFORMATION.

IN 1921 THE R-14 SUB RAN OUT OF FUEL WHILE AT SEA.

The sailors made sails out of blankets, curtain rods, and hammocks.

THEY SAILED 100 MILES (161 KM) AND MADE IT TO PORT IN HAWAII.

HAWAII

73

THE USS *NEW YORK'S* BOW WAS MADE WITH 7.5 TONS OF STEEL FROM THE FALLEN WORLD TRADE CENTER BUILDINGS.

The ship's motto is : "Strength forged through sacrifice. Never forget."

IT IS THE ONLY NAVY SHIP THAT HAS EIGHT-SIDED MASTS.

Advanced enclosed masts

IN 1855 THE U.S. ARMY IMPORTED CAMELS FOR BATTLE ON THE USS *SUPPLY* CAMEL CARRIER.

TO FIT THE CAMELS AND THEIR LARGE HUMPS, WORKERS CUT AWAY PART OF THE SHIP'S MAIN DECK.

THE CAMELS MADE IT TO THE UNITED STATES BUT WERE NEVER USED FOR BATTLE.

IN 1945 THE U.S. NAVY USED A REFRIGERATED BARGE TO DELIVER ICE CREAM TO NAVY SHIPS.

THE BARGE COULD MAKE 10 GALLONS (38 LITERS) OF ICE CREAM EVERY SEVEN MINUTES.

The barge went from ship to ship all over the Pacific Ocean.

Is it a BOAT or a PLANE ?

THE LUN WAS A MASSIVE GROUND EFFECT VEHICLE (GEV) WITH A 148-FOOT (45-METER) WINGSPAN.

IT USED THE AIR CURRENTS MADE BY ITS HUGE WINGS TO "FLY" ABOVE THE WATER'S SURFACE.

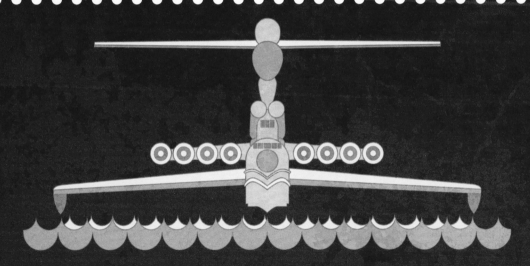

THE LUN HAD ONLY A LARGE HYDRO-SKI FOR LANDING.

SWCS STANDS FOR "SHALLOW WATER COMBAT SUBMERSIBLE."

THESE ARE "MINI-SUBS" FOR NAVY SEALS, A SPECIAL FORCES UNIT IN THE U.S. NAVY.

The SWCS deploys from a mothership and quickly and quietly allows SEALS to enter hostile lands.

The LCS is the U.S. Navy's newest class of warship.

Although the ships are small, they can go **40 KNOTS (46 MPH/74 KPH)!**

COMMANDER JOHN KOCHENDORFER CALLS IT, "THE COOLEST SHIP OUT THERE. A MILITARY JET SKI WITH A FLIGHT DECK AND A GUN."

The

USS VESUVIUS

served in the Spanish-American War (1898).
It was the only ship to use guns that shot

DYNAMITE.

ITS ONE **MAJOR FLAW** WAS THAT ITS GUNS WERE NOT ON SWIVELS. IF A SOLDIER WANTED TO REDIRECT A GUN'S AIM, THE **WHOLE SHIP** HAD TO MOVE.

ONLY **ONE** IX-529 WAS EVER BUILT. IT WAS THE WORLD'S FIRST **STEALTH SHIP.**

THE U.S. MILITARY NEVER REALLY USED THE *SEA SHADOW*. SO THEY SOLD IT FOR SCRAP IN 2012.

The ship in the James Bond movie *Tomorrow Never Dies* was based on the *Sea Shadow*.

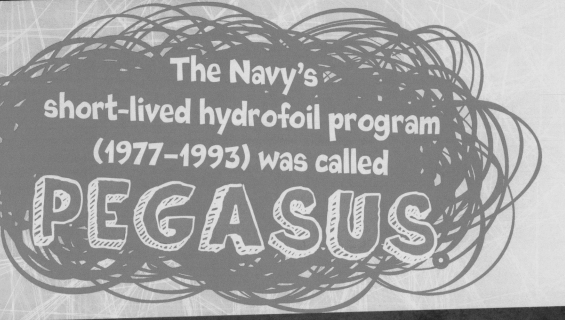

The Navy's short-lived hydrofoil program (1977–1993) was called **PEGASUS**.

WHEN "FOILBORNE" THE SHIP COULD GO MORE THAN 48 KNOTS (55 MPH/90 KPH)!

TO GO "FOILBORNE" THE SHIP'S HYDROFOILS (winglike structures) WOULD LIFT THE SHIPS INTO THE AIR.

DURING WORLD WAR II, THE BRITISH WANTED TO BUILD AN AIRCRAFT CARRIER WITH ICE AND WOOD PULP.

They made a model that was 30 feet (9 m) wide by 60 feet (18 m) long to test its **strength**.

THE MODEL WAS DURABLE. BUT FUNDING ISSUES CAUSED THE PROJECT TO FAIL.

THE FS *MARJATA* IS ONE OF THE WORLD'S TOP SPY SHIPS —AND IT'S SHAPED LIKE A

PIZZA SLICE!

RUSSIA

Its main job is to spy on the Russian military in the Arctic Sea.

IT'S SO SOPHISTICATED THAT NOT MANY PEOPLE REALLY KNOW EVERYTHING IT CAN DO.

WE DO KNOW THAT IT HAS THE MOST HIGH-TECH SPY GEAR AROUND.

THE MOST POWERFUL ICEBREAKER IS CURRENTLY BEING BUILT IN RUSSIA.

It will be able to break through ice that's 9.8 feet (3 m) thick!

ICEBREAKERS GLIDE ONTO ICE AND THEN USE THEIR WEIGHT TO BREAK THROUGH IT.

LET'S COMPARE:

BNS BARROSO

COUNTRY:	Brazil
YEAR IN SERVICE:	2008
SURFACE SPEED:	27 knots
RANGE:	4,063 miles (6,539 km)
WEAPONS:	missiles, guns, torpedoes

NAVAL CORVETTE WARSHIPS

VS. CNS BENGBU

China

2013

28 knots

2,300 miles (3,701 km)

missiles, guns, torpedoes

LET'S COMPARE:
LENGTHS OF NAVY SHIPS

860 FT
(262 M)

CARRIER

CHARLES DE GAULLE

NATION

AIRCRAFT CAPACITY

35-40

CREW

1,950

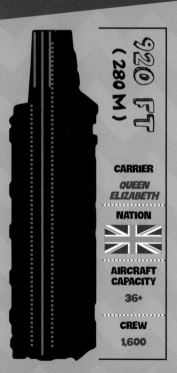

920 FT
(280 M)

CARRIER

QUEEN ELIZABETH

NATION

AIRCRAFT CAPACITY

36+

CREW

1,600

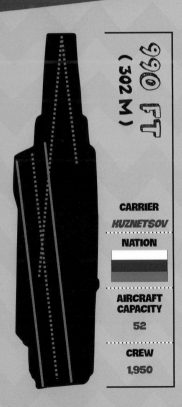

990 FT (302 M)

CARRIER

KUZNETSOV

NATION

AIRCRAFT CAPACITY

52

CREW

1,950

990 FT (302 M)

CARRIER

EX-VARYAG

NATION

AIRCRAFT CAPACITY

52

CREW

2,500

1,020 FT (311 M)

CARRIER

USS *GERALD R. FORD*

NATION

AIRCRAFT CAPACITY

75+

CREW

4,500

LET'S COMPARE:

INDIA'S FLEET

NATO Class	Engine Type	Fleet Size	Speed	Crew Size		
Chakra	☢	1	28-35 knots	73	131 yards (120 m)	
Sindhughosh	🌢	9	20 knots	52-68	82 yards (75 m)	
Shishumar	🌢	4	22.5 knots	73	66 yards (60 m)	

☢ Nuclear　　🌢 Diesel

INDIAN AND CHINESE SUBS

CHINA'S FLEET

NATO Class	Engine Type	Fleet Size	Speed	Crew Size		
Jin	☢	3	>20 knots	120	153 yards (140 m)	
Xia	☢	1	22 knots	140	131 yards (120 m)	
Shang	☢	2	30 knots	100	120 yards (110 m)	

HOVERCRAFTS RIDE ON A CUSHION OF AIR AND ARE MADE TO LAND TROOPS ON BEACHES.

Russia and Ukraine have the largest military hovercrafts. Each one can carry **THREE BATTLE TANKS!**

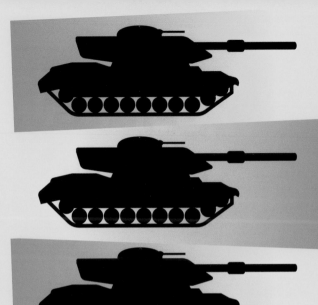

AT HIGH SPEEDS, MODERN HOVERCRAFTS LEAVE ALMOST NO WAKE.

HOSPITAL SHIPS
are giant moving
HOSPITALS.

U.S. NAVAL HOSPITAL SHIP
COMFORT

MILITARY HOSPITAL SHIPS HELP INJURED SOLDIERS. BUT THEY ALSO HELP PEOPLE ALL OVER THE WORLD IN NEED OF MEDICAL CARE.

THE USNS MERCY IS THE LENGTH OF THREE FOOTBALL FIELDS AND CONTAINS 1,000 BEDS.

U.S. NAVY SHIP LINGO
If you are on a Navy ship there are a few words you need to know:

BOW
the front of the ship

PORT
facing forward, the left-hand side of a ship

STARBOARD
facing forward, the right-hand side of a ship

STERN
the back of the ship

Some other terms:

MESS DECK
where you eat food

DECK
a level where you walk on the ship

THE HEAD
where you would find a toilet.

THE RACK
where you sleep

BULKHEADS
walls

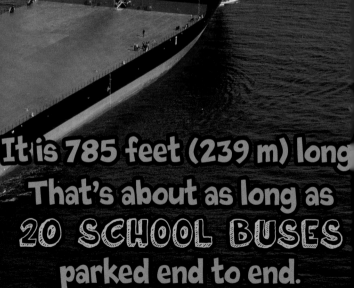

The *Montford Point* is an
80,000-TON
GIANT!

It is 785 feet (239 m) long
That's about as long as
20 SCHOOL BUSES
parked end to end.

DISASTER RELIEF AND ASSAULT OPERATIONS ARE JUST A COUPLE OF MONTFORD POINT'S DUTIES.

It acts as a floating port at sea; BOATS FROM ALL OVER come to get supplies, repair damages, trade troops, AND MORE.

During the American Revolutionary War (1775–1783), Great Britain docked old warships in New York Harbor to serve as PRISONS.

11,000 people died on these ships, many from DISEASE and MALNUTRITION.

THERE WERE NO FUNERALS FOR THIS LOT: MOST PEOPLE WERE SIMPLY TOSSED OVERBOARD WHEN THEY DIED.

It is estimated that **THOUSANDS OF RATS** also lived aboard these vessels.

THE FIRST SUB USED IN WARFARE
(the American Revolutionary War)

WAS CALLED
THE TURTLE.

To make it move, the operator used a **FOOT LEVER** and a **HAND CRANK.**

Its first job was to attach a time bomb to a British war ship. It failed.

BOOMERS carry and deliver **NUCLEAR WEAPONS.**

They are shaped like large fish, which allows them to move quickly and quietly in the water.

116

BOOMERS ARE **ALWAYS** ON PATROL.

USED IN WORLD WAR I (1914–1918), MARK 1 TANKS CAME IN TWO VERSIONS: THE "MALE" AND THE "FEMALE." (THE "MALE" TANK WEIGHED A LITTLE MORE.)

THE TANK WAS LOUD, AND FUMES FROM THE ENGINE OFTEN MADE THE CREW SICK!

It was such a beast of a **machine, it took** **FOUR** men to drive it.

The **BUSHMASTER** armored vehicle has **SPECIAL TIRES.** Even if the tires are **PUNCTURED, YOU CAN KEEP DRIVING.**

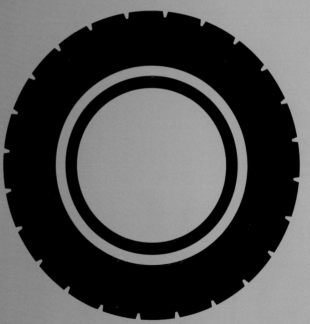

It can run for up to **three days** without stopping!

It takes only **ONE PERSON** to drive it. But it has room for up to **NINE MORE PEOPLE**.

Need a tow?
THE KETTENKRAD
could tow planes on an airstrip.

This machine was **HALF TANK/HALF MOTORCYCLE!** The Germans used it in World War II (1939–1945).

AFTER THE WAR, FARMERS USED IT AS AN ATV (ALL-TERRAIN VEHICLE).

The RhinoRunner was used to transport soldiers ON DANGEROUS ROADS DURING THE U.S. Iraq War (2003–2011).

124

This **VEHICLE** has survived 250 pounds (113 kilograms) of **EXPLOSIVES** detonated just 6.5 feet (2 meters) away!

People call it the "toughest bus on the planet."

USED IN WORLD WAR II, NOT MUCH IS KNOWN ABOUT THIS SMALL, ONE-MAN ROLLING TANK.

WHAT WE DO KNOW:

1) IT WAS MADE BY THE NAZIS.

2) THEY SHIPPED IT TO JAPAN.

3) IT WAS NEVER USED ON THE BATTLEFIELD.

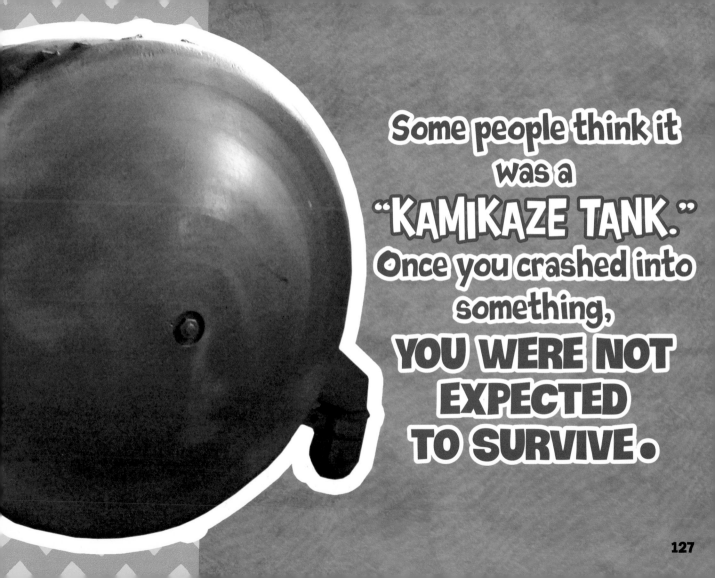

Some people think it was a **"KAMIKAZE TANK."** Once you crashed into something, **YOU WERE NOT EXPECTED TO SURVIVE.**

THE GUSTAV WAS THE HEAVIEST MOBILE ARTILLERY EVER BUILT. IT WEIGHED MORE THAN 1,300 TONS (1,180 METRIC TONS)!

The Gustav fired the HEAVIEST SHELLS of its day.

IT TOOK ALMOST **THREE** DAYS TO SET IT UP AND PREP IT FOR FIRING.

129

SOLDIERS PARACHUTED WITH THESE SCOOTERS

INTO ENEMY TERRITORY.

THE SCOOTERS COULD GO AS FAST AS 40 MILES (64 KILOMETERS) PER HOUR!

They could travel through 1 FOOT (0.3 M) of water.

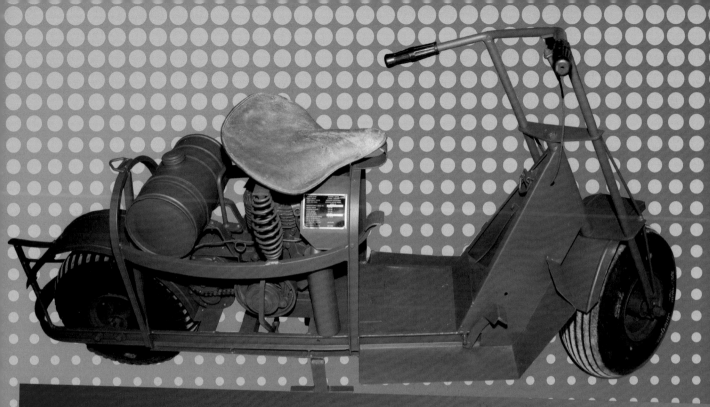

DO YOU WANT A CUSHMAN MODEL 53 SCOOTER? TODAY YOU CAN BUY A REFURBISHED ONE FOR ABOUT **$13,000.**

The Coyote armored vehicle is a high-tech spy machine.
THIS VEHICLE HAS:

radar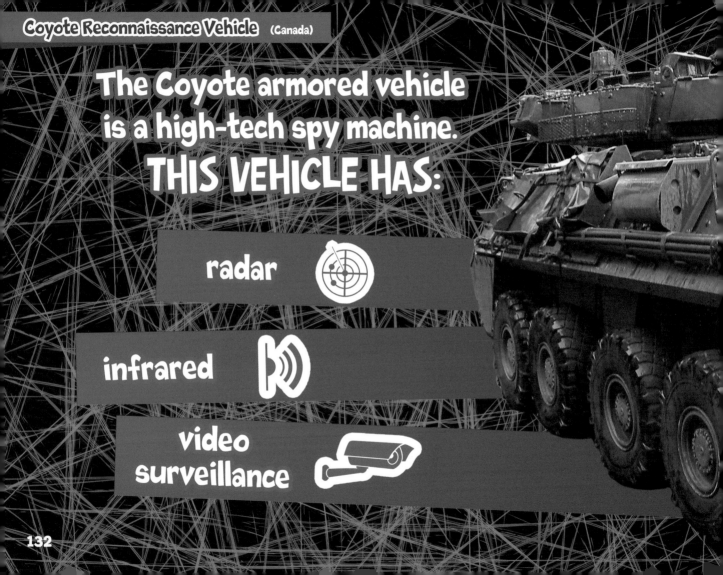

infrared

video surveillance

IT CAN DETECT VEHICLES UP TO 15 MILES (24 KM) AWAY.

THE COYOTE IS ONLY ABOUT 21 FEET (6 M LONG), BUT IT WEIGHS MORE THAN 14 TONS (13 METRIC TONS).

133

THE AARDVARK IS A MINE-FLAIL VEHICLE. IT CLEARS A PATH OF MINES BY DETONATING THEM.

SPECIAL SOUND-PROOFING IN THE CAB KEEPS THE CREW IN A NEAR-SILENT ENVIRONMENT.

The rear flail has **72 CHAINS** with striker tips.

CREWS ARE SAFE IN THIS BEAST!
No crew member in the vehicle has ever been hurt when flailing live mines.

Is the mission **TOO RISKY** for the average soldier? Send in the **BLACK KNIGHT!**

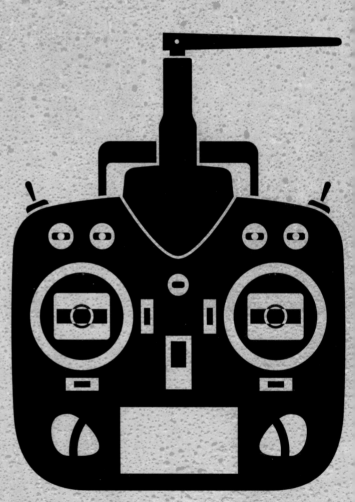

THE BLACK KNIGHT IS A UGCV: UNMANNED GROUND COMBAT VEHICLE.

Think you can hide? Not with this vehicle! It is a spying machine with video and thermal cameras.

SOLDIERS OPERATE IT KIND OF LIKE A REMOTE CONTROL CAR, BUT IT IS MUCH MORE ADVANCED.

During World War I, **RUSSIA** ordered Austin Armoured cars from **BRITAIN.**

THE SPOKES OF THE CARS WERE MADE OF WOOD.

The crew included a driver, a commander, and two gunners.

THE CAR HAD SMALL SLITS FOR **WINDOWS,** SO NONE OF THE CREW COULD SEE WELL.

The Vespa 150 TAP was made to be dropped from a plane: a two-person team would parachute with it!

If the machine blew out a tire in **ENEMY TERRITORY,** it had a spare stored in front of the **DRIVER'S SEAT.**

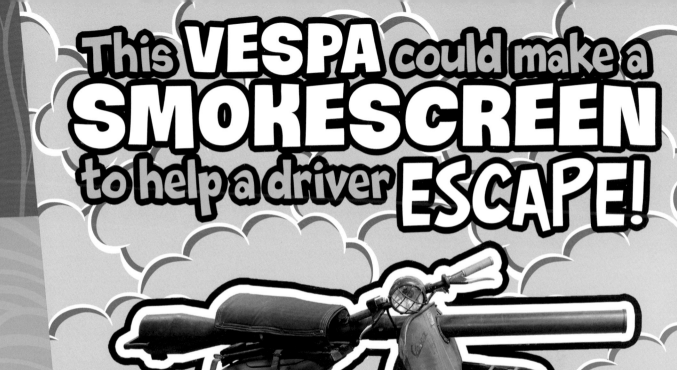

This VESPA could make a SMOKESCREEN to help a driver ESCAPE!

Designed for use in **WORLD WAR II,** the Weasel worked in **SNOW, WATER, AND MUD.**

to Berlin

U.S.A.
40185015-S

INSTALL DRAIN PLUGS IN HULL
BEFORE ATTEMPTING TO FLOAT

TWIN RUDDERS whisked the Weasel through **WATER.**

Muddy and wet areas were no match for **THE WEASEL!**

143

ASTROS can fire up to FIVE DIFFERENT KINDS of ROCKETS.

Unlike other vehicles of its kind, it can fire JET-POWERED CRUISE MISSILES.

144

AT 55 miles (88.5 km) per hour, THE ASTRO IS NO TURTLE IN THE FIELD!

THEY ARE SOMETIMES PUT ALONG THE COAST TO ACT AS A DEFENSE SYSTEM.

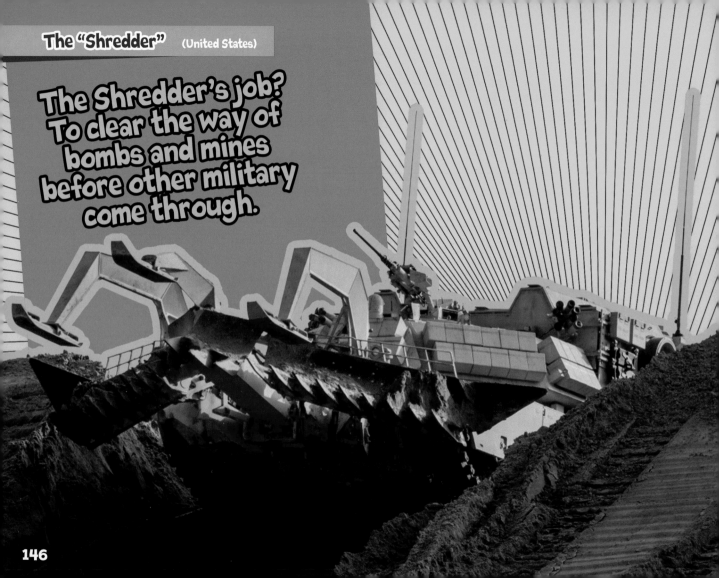

The "Shredder" (United States)

The Shredder's job? To clear the way of bombs and mines before other military come through.

THE SHREDDER WEIGHS **72 TONS** (65 METRIC TONS)! That's about as much as **36 CARS!**

ITS 3-TON PLOW is 15-feet (4.6-m) wide: the plow alone weighs as much as **THREE ASIAN ELEPHANTS!**

If you like remote control cars, **YOU'LL LOVE THE SHREDDER.** It can be run via remote control.

The DD TANK was nicknamed the DONALD DUCK TANK because it could operate in water.

IT COULD GO 21 MILES (34 KM) PER HOUR ON LAND

AND

4 KNOTS (ABOUT 4.6 MPH OR 7.4 KPH) AT SEA.

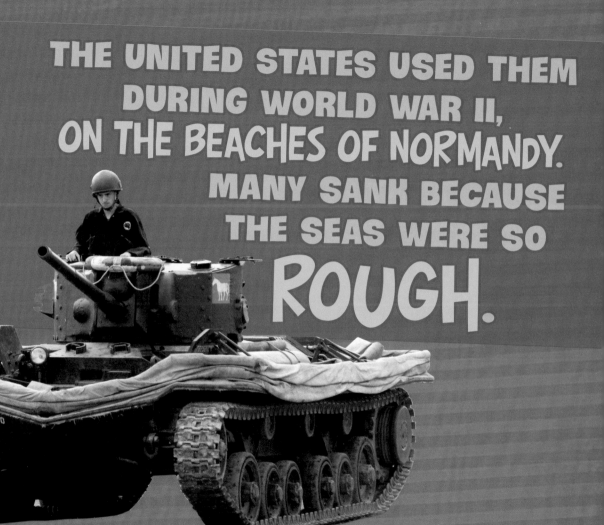

THE UNITED STATES USED THEM
DURING WORLD WAR II,
ON THE BEACHES OF NORMANDY.
MANY SANK BECAUSE
THE SEAS WERE SO
ROUGH.

BMW

made more than

36,000

R-12 motorcycles for the

GERMAN ARMY

in World War II.

THESE MOTORCYCLES WERE USED MOSTLY FOR SPYING AND DELIVERING NEWS AND MESSAGES.

YOU COULD ATTACH A SIDECAR AND A MACHINE GUN TO THEM TOO.

They were a **FAVORITE** on the front lines because of their **SPEED** and **MANEUVERABILITY.**

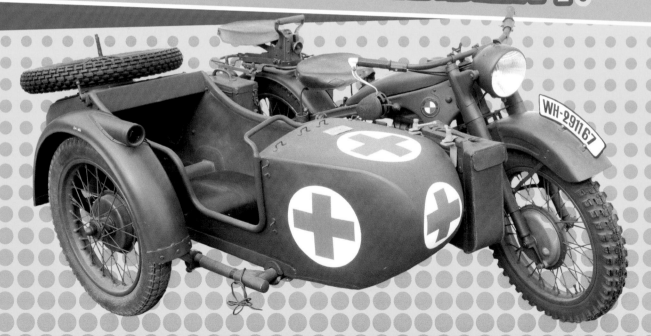

FACE OFF:

MODERN DAY
ANTI-AIRCRAFT
VEHICLES

COUNTRY:

YEAR IN SERVICE:

MAXIMUM SPEED (MPH/KPH):

FIREPOWER:

KTO ROSOMAK

Poland

2003

62 mph (100 kph)
1 autocannon
1 machine gun
6 smoke grenade dischargers

NORINCO TYPE 95

China

1999

34 mph (55 kph)
4 autocannons
8 smoke grenade dischargers

153

The **SCORPION** is like a **PUMPED-UP DUNE BUGGY.**

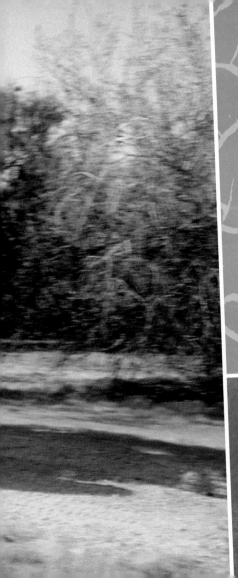

Navy SEALS and other soldiers have **ZIPPED** around in the Scorpion during desert wars.

IT CAN GO 200 MILES (322 KM) WITHOUT REFUELING.

Zaamurets was an armored **MILITARY TRAIN** built in Russia in 1916.

IT HAD TWO GUN TURRETS THAT COULD **SPIN ALL THE WAY AROUND** AND EIGHT MACHINE GUNS.

It weighed 130 tons (118 metric tons). That's as heavy as 60 CARS!

IT WAS SO **MASSIVE**, IT WAS CONSIDERED THE "KING OF THE MECHANICAL BEASTS."

THIS ARMORED CAR'S STRANGE ANGLES SHIELDED RIDERS FROM FLYING BULLETS.

The first **version** of these cars had **THREE TURRETS** for shooting at enemies.

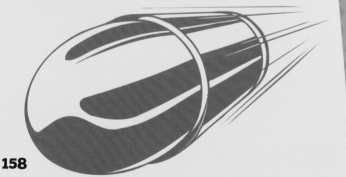

158

TO AIM THE GUNS, A COMMANDER WOULD HAVE TO **HAND CRANK** SPECIAL WHEELS TO **ROTATE** THE **TURRETS.**

159

MLRS = Multiple Launch Rocket System

The United States, France, Italy, West Germany, and the United Kingdom were all involved in its development.

Its ballistic missiles can hit targets **186 MILES (300 KM)** away. That's about as far as **WASHINGTON, D.C.** to **TRENTON, NJ!**

IT CAN FIRE 12 ROUNDS OF ROCKETS IN 40 SECONDS!

YOU DECIDE: MAKING PROGRESS?
TANKS THEN AND NOW

Early U.S. Tank:
The Ford Model M1918 Light Tank (1918)

Modern U.S. Tank:
The M1A1 Abrams

WEIGHT:
Ford: 3.3 tons (3 metric tons)
Abrams: 68 tons (62 metric tons)
(about 23 times heavier than the Ford tank!)

RANGE:

Ford: 34 miles (55 km)

Abrams: 265 miles (426 km)

(almost eight times farther than the Ford tank!)

MAXIMUM SPEED:

Ford: 8 mph (13 kph)

Abrams: 42 mph (68 kph)

(more than five times as fast as the Ford!)

VERDICT: PROGRESS MADE

NEED TO DIG A TRENCH FAST?

THE BTM-3 CAN DIG AN 800-METER (about a half-mile) TRENCH IN ONE HOUR!

IT ONLY TAKES 10 MINUTES TO GO FROM DRIVE MODE TO DIGGING MODE.

WHY WOULD YOU NEED A TRENCH? FOR UNDERCOVER COMMUNICATION OR DEFENSE.

Check out this remote-controlled surveillance and reconnaissance tool —the MAARS.

SEVEN

DIFFERENT KINDS OF SURVEILLANCE CAMERAS ARE PERCHED ON THIS ROBOT.

Besides spying, the MAARS can SET EXPLOSIVES, OPEN DOORS, and REMOVE UNWANTED OBJECTS with a special "claw."

Although the MAARS is totally high-tech, IT'S SUPER SLOW. Its maximum speed is 7 miles (11 km) per hour.

THE THING was a small, light tank built for the Vietnam War. Its goal: to blow up other tanks.

THE THING was only 12.5 feet (4 m) long by 8.5 feet (2 m) wide. THAT'S ABOUT THE LENGTH OF A MINI COOPER!

STILL, IT SOMEHOW COULD SQUISH THREE CREW MEMBERS INSIDE.

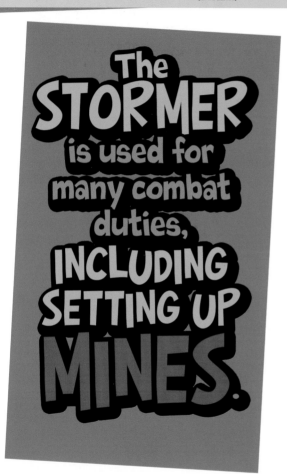

The STORMER is used for many combat duties, INCLUDING SETTING UP MINES.

IT TEARS UP THE ROAD AT 50 MILES (80 KM) PER HOUR.

ON WATER, IT MOVES AT ABOUT 3.1 MILES (5 KM) PER HOUR.

THE PROGVEV-T WAS A SOVIET-ERA TANK WITH A JET FIGHTER ENGINE ATTACHED.

The role of the jet engine: to blast away mines with its **HEAT.**

ITS PROBLEM? IT WAS **VERY HEAVY, VERY SLOW,** AND **VERY LOUD** (NOT TOO STEALTHY)!

173

The **GOLIATH**, made for World War II, was one of the first **REMOTE-CONTROLLED BATTLE VEHICLES**.

IT COULD CARRY MORE THAN 200 POUNDS (91 KG) OF EXPLOSIVES INTO BATTLE.

Think you'd be safe from it while hiding in a trench? Forget about it! THE GOLIATH COULD SCALE WALLS OF TRENCHES.

The South African-designed RG-33 MRAP first went into service in 2007.

IT COMES IN BOTH **4X4** AND **6X6** VERSIONS.

It can be used as an ambulance or a convoy escort.

It can also remove **EXPLOSIVES.**

Tsar Tank (Russia)

THE TSAR TANK OF WORLD WAR I LOOKED LIKE A GIGANTIC TRICYCLE.

It was one of the BIGGEST TANKS ever made. Its front wheels alone were 27 feet (8 m) in diameter! That's as long as four and a half grown men stacked END TO END!

During the tank's trial runs in 1915 it got stuck in the mud and no one could get it out.

It remained stuck in the mud for eight years until it was taken apart for scrap metal.

The United States made the Boarhound for the British Army to use in **World War II.**

THE BOARHOUND WAS A LARGE ARMORED CAR WITH EIGHT WHEELS. UP TO FIVE CREWMEN COULD FIT INSIDE.

THE BOARHOUND WAS MADE TO BE USED IN DESERT ENVIRONMENTS, LIKE NORTH AFRICA, WHERE SPEED AND SKILLFUL MOVEMENT WERE VERY IMPORTANT.

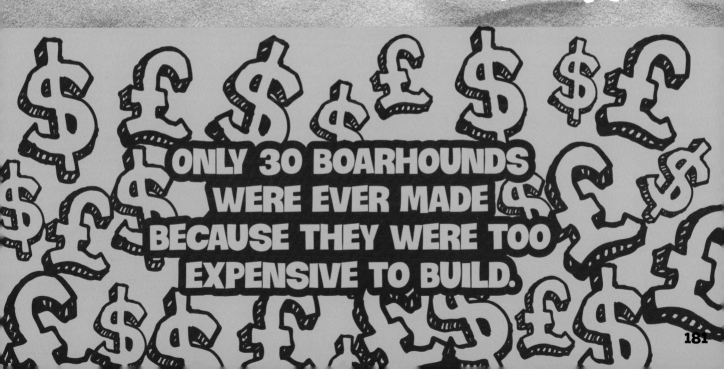

ONLY 30 BOARHOUNDS WERE EVER MADE BECAUSE THEY WERE TOO EXPENSIVE TO BUILD.

Playing tubas during battle? The Japanese War Tubas were built with acoustic locators that looked like tubas.

JAPANESE SOLDIERS MAY HAVE USED THIS MACHINE TO LISTEN FOR ENEMY PLANES DURING WORLD WAR I.

EARLY DETECTION OF ENEMY PLANES MEANT MORE TIME TO PREPARE FOR AN ATTACK.

Merkava (Israel)

WATCH OUT!

Unlike some tanks, a Merkava can fire at moving targets while moving.

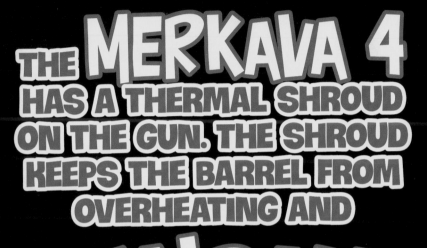

THE MERKAVA 4 HAS A THERMAL SHROUD ON THE GUN. THE SHROUD KEEPS THE BARREL FROM OVERHEATING AND **BENDING.**

THE SANDCAT IS USED BY SEVEN DIFFERENT COUNTRIES.

Its armor is made from steel and ceramic. The lightweight armor makes it a fast vehicle.

THE SANDCAT CAN BE STOCKED WITH A 40-MM AUTOMATIC GRENADE LAUNCHER, A 7.62 MM MACHINE GUN, OR A 12.7 MM MACHINE GUN.

YOU CAN ARM IT BY REMOTE CONTROL!

THE STRUMTIGER WAS A WORLD WAR II NAZI ROCKET LAUNCHER.

Loading the rocket was so tricky, it took five men to do it.

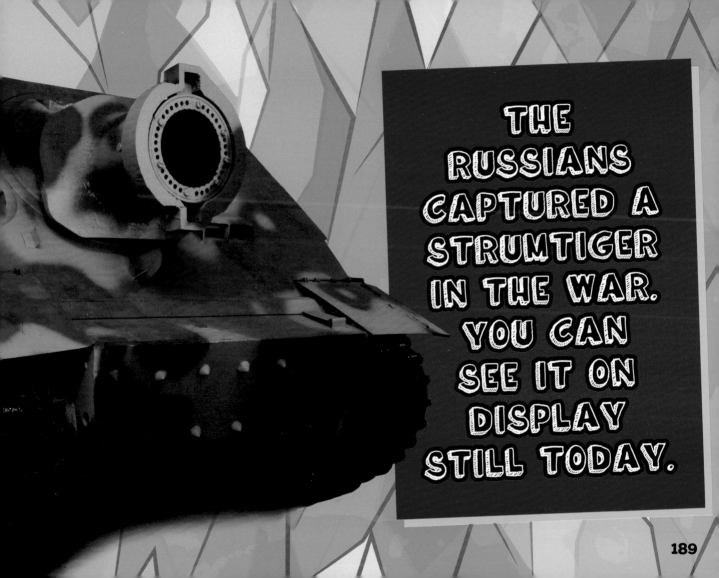

THE RUSSIANS CAPTURED A STRUMTIGER IN THE WAR. YOU CAN SEE IT ON DISPLAY STILL TODAY.

U.S. PARATROOPERS NOW CARRY FOLDABLE BIKES INTO ENEMY LANDS.

The bike can be folded up in 30 seconds.

WHY CARRY A BIKE? SOLDIERS ON BIKE CAN MOVE QUICKLY AND SILENTLY THROUGH ENEMY TERRITORY.

THE PARATROOPER BIKES CAN CARRY UP TO 500 POUNDS (227 KG) OF GEAR.

CHECK OUT
THIS ROUGH-TERRAIN MILITARY ROBOT!

BOSTON DYNAMICS
is working on a
rough-terrain robot called

BIG DOG
for the U.S. Army.

BIG DOG IS ABOUT 3 FEET (91 CM) LONG AND 2.5 FEET (76 CM) TALL.

IT CAN RUN AND WALK THROUGH RUBBLE, MUD, SNOW, DIRT, AND WATER.

193

FIAT 2000 Heavy Tank (Italy)

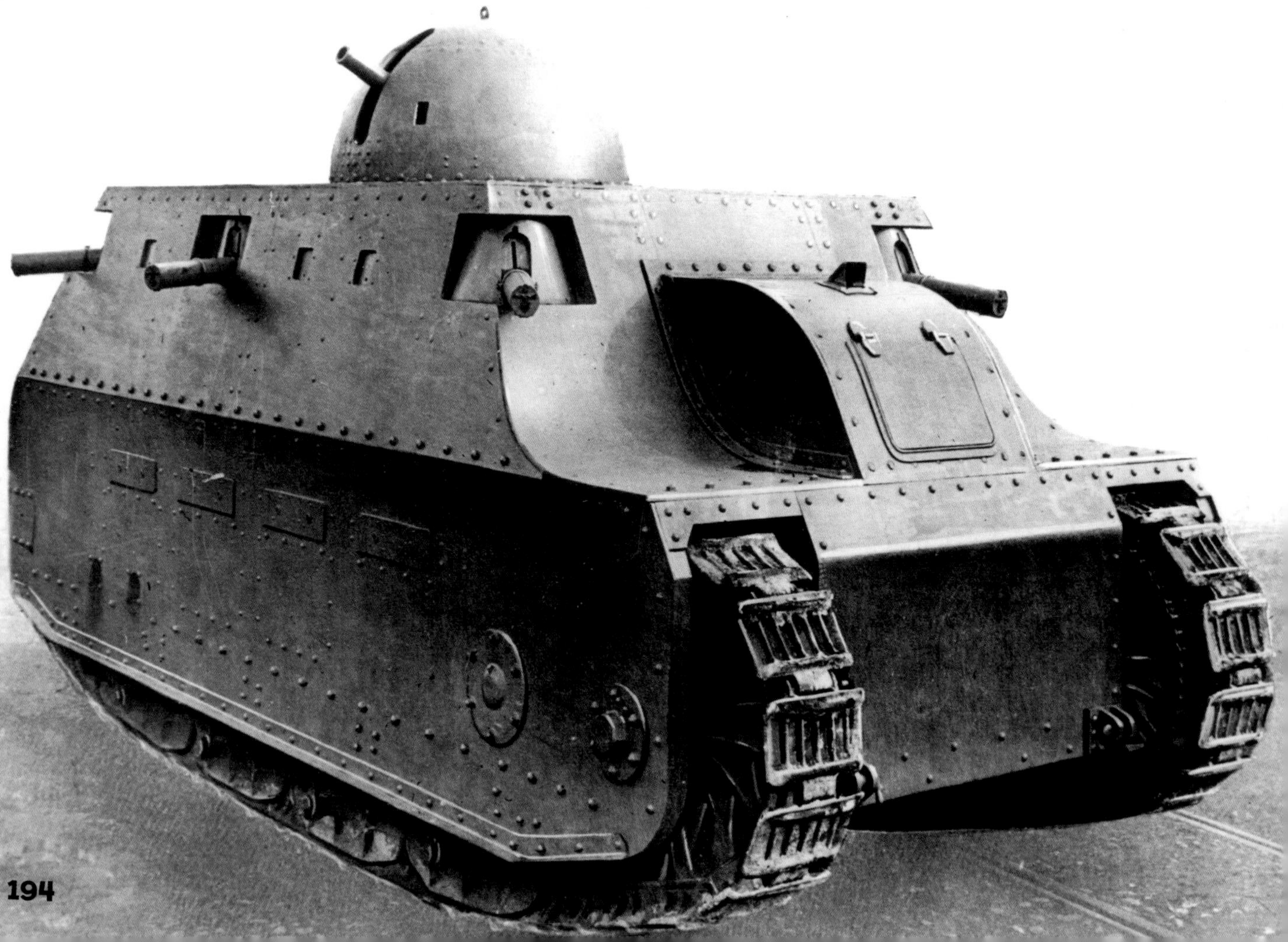

IT TOOK 10 MEN TO RUN THIS BEAST OF A TANK.

THE FIAT 2000 WAS CALLED THE PILLBOX BECAUSE OF ITS BOXY SHAPE.

It was used in WORLD WAR I, but only two were EVER MADE.

The NAMICA missile carrier can carry A WHOPPING EIGHT ready-to-fire missiles.

DON'T BLINK!
THIS BAD BOY LAUNCHES FOUR MISSILES IN ONE MINUTE!

THE MISSILES CAN EVEN BE FIRED IF THE TANK'S ENGINE IS POWERED OFF

THE HMMWV IS SHORT FOR HIGH MOBILITY MULTI-PURPOSE WHEELED VEHICLE. MOST PEOPLE KNOW THIS AS A HUMVEE.

THE HMMWV CAN CONQUER ALL KINDS OF TERRAIN —FROM JUNGLE TO DESERT!

NEED A LIFT FAST? THE HMMWV CAN BE MOVED IN A SLING VIA HELICOPTER.

Is the D-9R Dozer a tank or a bulldozer? BOTH!

THE ISRAELI ARMY USES ARMORED BULLDOZERS TO CLEAR AWAY RUBBLE IN **ANTI-TERRORISM OPERATIONS.**

A SOLDIER CAN OPERATE THIS ARMORED BULLDOZER BY REMOTE CONTROL!

IF SEARCHING AND DESTROYING IS THE JOB, THE GLADIATOR HAS IT COVERED!

THIS REMOTE VEHICLE CARRIES MINI-MISSILES AND GRENADE LAUNCHERS.

THE GLADIATOR HASN'T SEEN ANY BATTLE ACTION YET. IT'S STILL BEING DEVELOPED.

CHINESE

THE CHINESE USED WAR CHARIOTS AS EARLY AS **1200 BC.**

THE CHARIOTS WERE USED IN BATTLE, IN ROYAL HUNTS, AND TO MOVE SUPPLIES.

THE HITTITES USED CHARIOTS WITH A DRIVER AND A FIGHTER.

The fighter threw **JAVELINS** or used a **BOW AND ARROW** to thwart enemies.

THE HELEPOLIS WAS ONE OF THE FIRST ARMORED VEHICLES USED FOR FIGHTING.

The HELEPOLIS, used in the Siege of Rhodes, was the largest siege tower of the ancient world: 130 FEET (40 M) TALL and 65 FEET (20 M) WIDE. It was called "THE TAKER OF CITIES."

IT WAS COVERED IN SEAWEED AND ANIMAL SKINS TO MAKE IT FIREPROOF.

The Taker of Cities failed because it got stuck in the mud and couldn't be moved.

The M3 Stuart was first developed following World War I

MORE THAN 100 YEARS AGO.

But the Paraguay Army

STILL USES IT TODAY!

IT WAS NAMED AFTER THE U.S. CIVIL WAR CONFEDERATE GENERAL, J.E.B. STUART.

THIS TANK HAS BEEN USED ALL OVER THE WORLD IN MANY DIFFERENT CONFLICTS.

THE 2S35 KOALITSIYA-SV IS A KIND OF HOWITZER. IT'S A LONG-RANGE WEAPON.

210

NO CREW IS NEEDED INSIDE. One person can run it by remote control!

It has a higher rate of fire than any other artillery system. **IT CAN FIRE 16 ROUNDS PER MINUTE!**

THE M151 WAS NICKNAMED
THE MUTT
(MILITARY UTILITY TACTICAL TRUCK).

Unlike other military Jeeps, this one was not sold to the public. IT ROLLED OVER TOO EASILY.

An Army report claimed that the M151 was involved in 3,538 ACCIDENTS in the span of one year!

AN EGG-SHAPED "BLAST BUCKET" HOLDS THE ULTRA AP'S CREW UP TOP.

THE BLAST BUCKET PROTECTS SOLDIERS IN CASE OF A ROLLOVER OR ENEMY FIRE.

The Ultra AP is a prototype. It has not seen combat yet.

THE FOX WAS A CANADIAN-DEVELOPED ARMORED VEHICLE. IT WAS USED IN **WORLD WAR II** AND THE **PORTUGUESE COLONIAL WAR.**

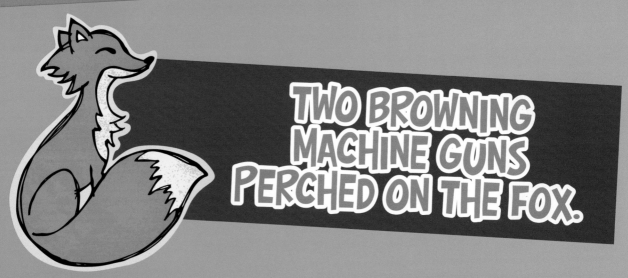

TWO BROWNING MACHINE GUNS PERCHED ON THE FOX.

PARTS OF THE RETIRED FOX WERE RECYCLED AND USED ON ANOTHER COMBAT VEHICLE: THE SABRE TANK.

LOOKING FOR A NEW RIDE? YOU CAN BUY A REFURBISHED FOX TODAY FOR ABOUT $30,000.

THE BEAVERETTE WAS A LIGHT-ARMORED CAR DESIGNED TO DEFEND BRITISH AIRFIELDS.

Its armor was created from flat sheets of steel.

THE BEAVERETTE HAD TINY WINDOWS. SOME SAY THE DRIVER NEEDED A SECOND GUY TO STICK HIS HEAD OUT THE TOP AND TELL HIM WHERE TO GO.

THE M1249 IS A BEEFED-UP TOW TRUCK.

It can tow disabled
vehicles weighing up to
**41 TONS
(37 METRIC TONS)!**

When a tank breaks down,
**THE M1249 COMES TO
THE RESCUE.**

ESCORT WAGONS FOR THE... MILITARY?

Wagons towed by horses and mules were common military vehicles during the Civil War (1861–1865).

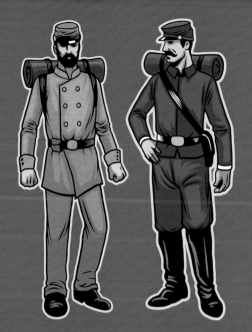

THE WHEELS EACH HAD 16 SPOKES, MAKING THEM VERY STRONG.

THE ESCORT WAGON WAS USED TO TRANSPORT TROOPS.

WHOA!
This is the BIG DADDY!

The T28 was the biggest tank ever made by the United States.

WHEN FULLY LOADED WITH WEAPONS, IT WEIGHED ABOUT 95 TONS (86 METRIC TONS). THAT'S ABOUT THE WEIGHT OF 75 POLAR BEARS!

SOME OF ITS ARMOR WAS 12 INCHES (30 CM) THICK.

BECAUSE OF ITS WEIGHT, THE T28 WAS SUPER SLOW! IT TOPPED OUT AT JUST 8 MILES (13 KM) PER HOUR.

THE PUNISHER IS A MILITARY MEGA-MONSTER!

TOPPING OUT AT 93 MILES PER HOUR (150 KPH). IT'S THE FASTEST TROOP CARRIER IN THE WORLD.

PUT THE PEDAL TO THE METAL!

IN JUST 10 SECONDS, THE PUNISHER CAN GO FROM 0 TO 60 MILES PER HOUR (97 KPH)!

Like a chameleon, the PL-01 can blend in to its infrared surroundings by CHANGING THE TEMPERATURE OF ITS OUTSIDE ARMOR.

THIS MAKES IT INVISIBLE TO INFRARED DETECTION SYSTEMS.

This tank is currently being built and is estimated to be in service by 2020.

LOOKING FOR JUST THE RIGHT VEHICLE?

THE OCELOT IS A TRANSFORMER. IT CAN CHANGE INTO A TRUCK, AN AMBULANCE, AND A NUMBER OF OTHER VEHICLES.

IT'S MADE TO TAKE BLASTS FROM BOMBS AND IEDS (Improvised Explosive Devices).

The
COMBAT GUARD
is called
"THE WORLD'S
ULTIMATE
4 X 4 VEHICLE."

Most ATVs can climb **40- TO 50-DEGREE SLOPES.** But the Combat Guard can tackle **70-DEGREE SLOPES!**

ITS MASSIVE TIRES ARE 54 INCHES (137 CM) HIGH! THAT'S PROBABLY TALLER THAN YOU!

GLOSSARY

acoustic locators—machines that detect the sounds of aircraft

airships—a large aircraft that does not have wings but has a body filled with gas (like helium or hydrogen) so that it floats

anti-terrorism—the practice, tactics, and strategy military agencies use to fight or prevent terrorism

assault vehicles—armed vehicles that are used to attack or defend

blimps—types of airships

classified information— information that only top military people know

emblems—a person or thing used to represent something

flail—a mine flail is a tool that clears a safe path through a mine field by setting off the mines on purpose

flytime—how long an airplane can fly without stopping to refuel

ground-based sensors—computer systems on land that can find and locate ships and airplanes

howitzer—a short gun used to fire shells

hydrofoil—a fast boat that rises up out of the water when it reaches high speeds

icebreakers—large boats that cut through thick ice

infrared—rays of light that cannot be seen

Mach—a unit of measurement for speeds faster than the speed of sound

malfunction—when something does not work as it is supposed to

malnutrition—when a person's body doesn't get the right vitamins and nutrients

mothership—a ship or airplane that carries smaller ships or airplanes

NATO—the abbreviation for North Atlantic Treaty Organization, a coalition of 28 countries that help each other with defense

operational checks—all of the things people need to do to make sure everything is working on a boat

prototype—a first model of something

ramjet—a type of jet engine where the air is sucked in and compressed by the forward motion of the airplane

range—the maximum distance ammunition can travel to reach its target; or the distance that a vehicle can travel without refueling

reconnaissance—a mission where soldiers go to find out details about an enemy

refurbish—to repair

shroud—something used to hide or shield something

siege tower—a type of vehicle built to withstand attack while trying to breach defensive walls

sophisticated—complex

supersonic—faster than the speed of sound

surveillance—the act of keeping very close watch on someone, someplace, or something

thermal camera—a camera that can take pictures in the dark based on the heat signature of objects

turret—the part on a military vehicle from which guns are fired

ABOUT THE AUTHOR

Cari is the author of more than 150 books for young readers, including the Tiny series (Penguin Books for Young Readers) and the Flash Forward Fairy Tale series (Scholastic). She lives in Edwards, Colorado, with her husband John, four sons, one horse, and one dog. Cari loves to visit schools and libraries. You can find out more at www.carimeister.com.

LOOKING FOR MORE TOTALLY WACKY TRIVIA?

INDEX

Mind Benders are published by Capstone,
1710 Roe Crest Drive, North Mankato, Minnesota 56003
www.mycapstone.com

Editors: Megan Atwood and Megan Peterson
Designer: Kyle Grenz
Media Researcher: Jo Miller
Production Specialist: Tori Abraham

Library of Congress Cataloging-in-Publication Data
Library of Congress Cataloging-in-Publicaton data is available on the Library of Congress website.
ISBN: 978-1-5157-4542-6 (paperback)
Summary: Readers will learn over 200 facts about military sea, air, and land vehicles, such as helicopters and stealth flighters, submarines and mammoth ships, and tanks and motorcycles. Readers will love the unusual facts, the amazing colorful spreads, and the lively photos attached to each vehicle's information.

Photo Credits
Alamy: Andrew Kitching, 142, Chronicle, 194, Colin C. Hill, 149, CPC Collection, 213, Ian Nellist, 131, INTERFOTO, 27, 151, iWebbstock, 121, Mihai Popa, 186, PF-(aircraft), 61, PF-(sdasm3), 28, Stocktrek Images/Daniele Faccioli, 31, Sueddeutsche Zeitung Photo, 129, War Archive, 18; AP Images: U.S. Army, 38; CriaImages.com: Jay Robert Nash Collection, 110; Gamma-Rapho via Getty Images: Reporters Associes, 63; Getty Images: Archive Photos/ Buyenlarge/Bain News Service, 157, Bettmann, 26, 37, 50, De Agostini Picture Library, 205 (top left), SSPL/Florilegius, 204, TASS, 80, The LIFE Images Collection/Carl Mydans/Contributor, 209, The LIFE Images Collection/ Greg Mathieson/Mai, 154, The LIFE Picture Collection/Ralph Crane, 4; Glow Images: Deposit Photos, 66; Library of Congress, 208 (inset), 222; NARA, 26-27 (background);NASA, 14, 15; Newscom: akg-images, 36, Peter Connolly, 207 (right), EPA/Ali Haider, 124, European Press Agency/Sergel_Supinsky, 41, Everett Collection, 7 (right), 113, Heritage Images/Ann Ronan Picture Library, 16, Hilary Jane Morgan, 17 (left), KRT HANDOUT, 166, Reuters/Andrew Innerarity, 29, Reuters/Robert Kolek, 40, Tass Photos/Zarembo Igor Itar, 104, WENN/JP5/ZOB/BigDog image courtesy of Boston Dynamics ©2009, 19, Xinhua News Agency/Chen Rui, 23, Xinhua News Agency/Jia Yuchen, 210, ZUMA Press/EPN/Dong-Min Jang, 52 (F-15K), ZUMA Press/Keystone Pictures USA, 91, ZUMA Press/TASS, 97, Nova Development Corporation, 100-101 (flags), 138 (flags); NY Daily News Archive via Getty Images/Joe Petrella, 39; Photo by REX: Shutterstock, 135; Shutterstock: 13ree.design, 109 (bottom right), 3DMaestro, 67, aarrows, 130, admin_design, 53 (South Korea flag), advent, 51, Alfredo Cerra, 74, Arcady, 125, Art tools, 183, B Calkins, 78 (background), Bascar, 180 (bottom), bazzier, 223 (left), bekulnis, 130, BOONROONG, 203, Brian Goff, 93, caesart, 150, Carsten Reisinger, 208 (flag), Color Brush, 207 (left), Dashikka, 227 (top), dedek, 3 (killer whale), Demeshko Alexandr, 65 (submarine), 102-103 (submarines), dreamnikon, 52 (F-15CJ/DJ), Dxinerz-Pvt-Ltd, 132 (middle), Dxinerz-Pvt-Ltd, 161 (left), Edoma, 122, Elena Terletskaya, 77 (top), Everett Historical, 64, 152-153 (background), Fat Jackey, 200, Flik47, 184, Frank Fennema, 223 (right), Gaulois_s, 94 (bottom), gdinny, 188-189 (background), Getmilitaryphotos, 83, Good Vector, 158, HedgehogVector, 105, Hurst Photo, 5 (bottom), i4lcocl2, 171, i4lcocl2, 171, Iakov Filimonov, 76, iDesign, 227 (bottom), Ivan Kotliar, 86, Jacky Co, 55, Jane Kelly, 17 (left), konahinab, 56 (wings), kontur-vid, 132 (bottom), 137, Leremy, 123, Lilu330, 177, LINE ICONS, 48 (top), Liudmyia Marykon, 47 (UFOs), LoopAll, 119 (top), Lukasz Stefanski, 180 (top), lukpedclub, 46 (pancake), mariocigic, 107 (background), Marzolino, 77 (bottom), mavi, 73 (bottom), Miceking, 167, Mikadun, 123 (background), Mike McDonald, 216, Milos Kontic, 22, momojung, 94 (top), Mr.Creative, 161 (right), MSPhotographic, 73 (top), Naci Yavuz, 7 (left), NEGOVURA, 109 (top left), Panda Vector, 132, (top), Pakhnyushchy, 111, PILart, 108, PLRANG ART, 153 (left), RedlineVector, 173, Regular, 148 (background), Robert Spriggs, 159, Roman Sotola, 136, SFerdon, 119 (bottom), shtiel, 19, Skalapendra, 46 (wings), Sloth Astronaut, 112, SoRad, 25, stockphoto mania, 138 (wood), StudioIcon, 72 (top), Svetlana Guteneva, 109 (top right), THPStock, 28 (background), Thumbelina, 3 (tank), Toozedesign, 228, tovovan, 57, Tribalium, 205 (bottom left), Tsibii Lesia, 53 (USA, China, Japan, Vietnam, and Russia flags), VectorPlotnikoff, 106, Venomous Vector, 120, Vladvm, 109 (bottom left), Volina, 79, Voropaev Vasiliy, 147 (right), woverwolf, 205 (bottom right), Yayayoyo, 145; The Image Works/RIA-Novosti, 189; U.S. Air Force photo by Master Sgt. Andy Dunaway, 10, Master Sgt. Kevin J. Gruenwald, 32, Osakabe Yasuo, 2, 3 (top), Senior Airman Brian Ferguson, 42, Senior Airman Chris Massey, 52 (F-22A), Staff Sgt. Aaron Allmon, cover (top right), 33, Staff Sgt. Bennie J. Davis III, back cover (top left), 34, 35, Staff Sgt. Courtney Richardson, 106, Tech. Sgt. Justin D. Pyle, 43, Tech. Sgt. Robert J. Horstman, 8, Master Sgt. Greg Steele, 9; U.S. Army Photo by Capt. Tania Donovan, 199, Denise DeMonia, 20, Maj. Christopher Thomas, 44, Sgt. Scott Davis, 220, Spc. Randis Monroe, 45, Staff Sgt. Bryanna Poulin, 21; U.S. Marine Corps Photo by Lance Cpl. Preston McDonald, 146, Lance Cpl. William Hester, cover (top left); U.S. Navy photo, cover (bottom left), Lt. Jan Shultis, 84, MC1 Jeffrey Jay Price, 70, MC2 Brian Caracci, 12, MC2 Jillian Lotti, 24, MC3 Mark Andrew Hays, 75, OS2 John Bouvia, 68, Petty Officer 2nd Class Ronald Gutridge, 117, PH3 Rodney W. Jones, 13, courtesy of General Dynamics, 106, courtesy of Naval Sea Systems Command, 88; Wikimedia, 56, 182, Ajai Shukla, 197, Alex Beltyukov, 52 (T-50), Alf van Beem, back cover (bottom left), 141, Allocer, 128, Articseahorse, 176, Azurri13579, 52 (SU-30MKV), Bernhard Gröhl, 127, Chikumaya, 190, Dmitriy Pichugin, 52 (SU-27SK), DoD photo by: TECH. SGT. H. H. DEFFNER, 144, FOX 52, 100, GFDL, 6, Kaboldy, 60, Janez Novak, Ljubljana, Slovenija, 165, LOC/Bain News Service, 118, Mark Holloway, 225, Max Smith, 153 (right), Max Smith, 218, Mike from Vancouver, Canada, 132-133, NARA, 87, National Archives, back cover (right), 5 (top), Randen Pederson, cover (bottom right), SSGT REYNALDO RAMON, USAF, 48 (bottom), 49, SSG Richard Hart, 160, The source Unknown, 139, Unknown, 178, U.S. Naval Historical Center, 72 (bottom), U.S. Army, 175, U.S. Navy, 47, 58, XaHyMaH, 30, User:J JMesserly, 172, USMC Archives from Quantico, USA, 168

Design Elements by Capstone and Shutterstock

Printed in Canada.
010037S17